365 DAY

NOTEBOOK

_____

_____

_____

JANUARY

1

_____

_____

_____

_____

_____

_____

_____

_____

_____

_____

_____

_____

_____

_____

_____

_____

JANUARY

2

JANUARY

3

JANUARY

4

JANUARY

5

JANUARY

6

_____
_____
_____
_____
_____
_____
_____
_____
_____
_____
_____
_____
_____
_____
_____
_____
_____
_____

JANUARY

7

JANUARY

8

JANUARY

9

JANUARY

10

_____
_____
_____
_____
_____
_____
_____
_____
_____
_____
_____
_____
_____
_____
_____
_____
_____

JANUARY

11

JANUARY

12

JANUARY

13

JANUARY

14

JANUARY

15

JANUARY

16

_____
_____
_____
_____
_____
_____
_____
_____
_____
_____
_____
_____
_____
_____
_____
_____
_____

JANUARY

17

JANUARY

18

JANUARY

19

JANUARY

20

JANUARY

21

JANUARY

22

JANUARY
23

JANUARY

24

JANUARY
25

JANUARY

26

JANUARY

27

JANUARY

28

JANUARY
29

JANUARY

30

JANUARY
31

FEBRUARY

1

FEBRUARY

2

FEBRUARY

3

FEBRUARY

4

FEBRUARY

5

FEBRUARY

6

_____

_____

_____

_____

_____

_____

_____

_____

_____

_____

_____

_____

_____

_____

_____

_____

FEBRUARY

7

FEBRUARY

8

FEBRUARY
9

FEBRUARY
10

FEBRUARY

11

FEBRUARY

12

FEBRUARY

13

FEBRUARY

14

FEBRUARY

15

FEBRUARY

16

FEBRUARY
17

FEBRUARY

18

FEBRUARY

19

FEBRUARY

20

FEBRUARY

21

FEBRUARY

22

FEBRUARY

23

FEBRUARY

24

FEBRUARY

25

FEBRUARY

26

FEBRUARY
27

FEBRUARY

28

FEBRUARY
29

MARCH

1

MARCH

2

MARCH

3

MARCH

4

MARCH

5

MARCH

6

MARCH

7

MARCH

8

MARCH

9

MARCH

10

MARCH

11

MARCH

12

MARCH

13

MARCH

14

MARCH

15

MARCH
16

MARCH

17

MARCH

18

MARCH

19

_____
_____
_____
_____
_____
_____
_____
_____
_____
_____
_____
_____
_____
_____
_____
_____
_____
_____

MARCH

20

MARCH

21

MARCH

22

MARCH

23

MARCH

24

MARCH

25

MARCH

26

_____
_____
_____
_____
_____
_____
_____
_____
_____
_____
_____
_____
_____
_____
_____
_____
_____
_____

MARCH

27

MARCH

28

MARCH
29

_____

_____

_____

_____

_____

_____

_____

_____

_____

_____

_____

_____

_____

_____

_____

_____

_____

_____

MARCH

30

MARCH

31

APRIL

1

APRIL

2

APRIL

3

APRIL

4

APRIL

5

APRIL

6

APRIL

7

APRIL

8

APRIL

9

APRIL

10

APRIL

11

APRIL

12

APRIL

13

APRIL

14

APRIL

15

APRIL

16

APRIL

17

_____
_____
_____
_____
_____
_____
_____
_____
_____
_____
_____
_____
_____
_____
_____
_____
_____
_____

APRIL

18

APRIL

19

APRIL

20

APRIL

21

APRIL

22

APRIL

23

_____
_____
_____
_____
_____
_____
_____
_____
_____
_____
_____
_____
_____
_____
_____
_____
_____

APRIL

24

APRIL

25

APRIL

26

APRIL

27

APRIL

28

_____
_____
_____
_____
_____
_____
_____
_____
_____
_____
_____
_____
_____
_____
_____
_____
_____
_____
_____
_____

APRIL

29

APRIL

30

MAY

1

_____

_____

_____

_____

_____

_____

_____

_____

_____

_____

_____

_____

_____

_____

MAY

2

MAY

3

MAY

4

MAY
5

MAY

6

MAY

7

MAY

8

MAY

9

MAY

10

MAY

11

MAY

12

MAY

13

_____
_____
_____
_____
_____
_____
_____
_____
_____
_____
_____
_____
_____
_____
_____

MAY

14

MAY

15

_____
_____
_____
_____
_____
_____
_____
_____
_____
_____
_____
_____
_____
_____
_____
_____
_____
_____
_____

MAY
16

MAY

17

MAY

18

MAY

19

MAY

20

MAY

21

MAY

22

MAY

23

MAY

24

MAY

25

MAY

26

MAY

27

MAY

28

M A Y

29

MAY
30

MAY

31

JUNE

1

JUNE

2

JUNE

3

JUNE

4

JUNE

5

JUNE

6

JUNE

7

JUNE

8

JUNE

9

_____
_____
_____
_____
_____
_____
_____
_____
_____
_____
_____
_____
_____
_____
_____
_____
_____
_____
_____
_____
_____
_____

JUNE

10

JUNE

11

JUNE

12

JUNE

13

JUNE

14

JUNE

15

JUNE
16

JUNE

17

JUNE

18

JUNE

19

JUNE
20

JUNE

21

JUNE

22

JUNE

23

JUNE

24

JUNE

25

JUNE
26

JUNE

27

JUNE
28

JUNE

29

JUNE
30

_____
_____
_____
_____
_____
_____
_____
_____
_____
_____
_____
_____
_____
_____
_____
_____
_____
_____

JULY

1

JULY

2

JULY

3

JULY

4

JULY

5

JULY

6

JULY

7

JULY

8

JULY

9

JULY

10

JULY

11

JULY

12

_____
_____
_____
_____
_____
_____
_____
_____
_____
_____
_____
_____
_____
_____
_____
_____

JULY

13

JULY

14

JULY

15

JULY

16

_____

_____

_____

_____

_____

_____

_____

_____

_____

_____

_____

_____

_____

_____

_____

_____

_____

_____

JULY

17

JULY

18

JULY

19

JULY

20

JULY

21

JULY

22

JULY

23

JULY

24

JULY

25

JULY

26

JULY

27

JULY

28

JULY

29

JULY

30

JULY

31

AUGUST

1

AUGUST

2

AUGUST

3

AUGUST

4

AUGUST

5

AUGUST

6

AUGUST

7

AUGUST

8

AUGUST

9

AUGUST
10

AUGUST
11

AUGUST

12

AUGUST

13

AUGUST

14

AUGUST

15

AUGUST

16

AUGUST
17

AUGUST

18

AUGUST

19

AUGUST

20

AUGUST
21

AUGUST

22

AUGUST

23

AUGUST

24

AUGUST

25

AUGUST

26

AUGUST

27

AUGUST
28

AUGUST

29

AUGUST

30

AUGUST

31

SEPTEMBER

1

SEPTEMBER

2

SEPTEMBER

3

SEPTEMBER

4

SEPTEMBER

5

SEPTEMBER

6

SEPTEMBER

7

SEPTEMBER

8

SEPTEMBER

9

SEPTEMBER

10

SEPTEMBER

11

SEPTEMBER

12

SEPTEMBER

13

SEPTEMBER

14

SEPTEMBER

15

SEPTEMBER

16

SEPTEMBER
17

SEPTEMBER

18

SEPTEMBER

19

SEPTEMBER

20

SEPTEMBER

21

_____

_____

_____

_____

_____

_____

_____

_____

_____

_____

_____

_____

_____

_____

_____

_____

_____

SEPTEMBER

22

SEPTEMBER

23

SEPTEMBER

24

SEPTEMBER

25

SEPTEMBER

26

SEPTEMBER

27

SEPTEMBER
28

SEPTEMBER

29

SEPTEMBER

30

OCTOBER

1

OCTOBER

2

OCTOBER

3

OCTOBER

4

OCTOBER
5

OCTOBER

6

OCTOBER

7

OCTOBER

8

OCTOBER
9

OCTOBER

10

OCTOBER
11

OCTOBER

12

OCTOBER

13

OCTOBER

14

OCTOBER

15

OCTOBER

18

OCTOBER

17

OCTOBER

18

OCTOBER

19

OCTOBER

20

OCTOBER

21

OCTOBER

22

OCTOBER
23

OCTOBER

24

OCTOBER
25

OCTOBER

26

OCTOBER

27

OCTOBER

28

OCTOBER

29

OCTOBER
30

OCTOBER
31

NOVEMBER
1

NOVEMBER

2

NOVEMBER

3

NOVEMBER
4

NOVEMBER

5

NOVEMBER

6

NOVEMBER

7

NOVEMBER

8

NOVEMBER

9

NOVEMBER

10

NOVEMBER

11

NOVEMBER

12

NOVEMBER

13

NOVEMBER

14

NOVEMBER

15

NOVEMBER

16

NOVEMBER
17

NOVEMBER

18

NOVEMBER

19

NOVEMBER

20

NOVEMBER

21

NOVEMBER

22

NOVEMBER

23

NOVEMBER
24

NOVEMBER

25

NOVEMBER

26

NOVEMBER

27

NOVEMBER

28

NOVEMBER

29

NOVEMBER

30

DECEMBER

1

DECEMBER

2

DECEMBER

3

DECEMBER

4

DECEMBER

5

DECEMBER

6

DECEMBER

7

DECEMBER

8

DECEMBER

9

DECEMBER

10

DECEMBER

11

DECEMBER

12

DECEMBER

13

DECEMBER

14

DECEMBER

15

DECEMBER

16

DECEMBER

17

DECEMBER

18

DECEMBER

19

DECEMBER

20

DECEMBER

21

DECEMBER

22

DECEMBER

23

DECEMBER

24

DECEMBER

25

DECEMBER

26

DECEMBER

27

DECEMBER

28

DECEMBER

29

DECEMBER

30

DECEMBER
31